THE YANADIS
OF
SOUTHERN INDIA

THE YANADIS
OF
SOUTHERN INDIA

T. RANGA RAO

GYAN

Published by

GYAN

Gyan Publishing House
5, Ansari Road
Daryaganj, New Delhi-110002
Phone: 011-47034999, 9811692060
E-mail: books@gyanbooks.com

Distribution Network
gyanbooks.com
India, USA, Canada, UK, Australia, France

ISBN : 978-81-212-4235-6 (PB)
First Published, Kanigiri, 1899

2nd Impression 2020

Printed at: Gyan Press, Delhi.

The Yanadis of Southern India
Author: T. Ranga Rao

THE YANADIS

OF

SOUTHERN INDIA

BY

T. RANGA RAO,

PRINTED AT THE S. R. V. BRANCH PRESS, KANIGIRI.

1899.

PREFATORY NOTE.

The story of the Yanadis, already before the public, is neither full, nor up to date. Their manners and customs are slowly changing, their habits of life are altering. The accounts given of them some thirty years ago are not only inadequate but not quite accurate. In this paper, an attempt is made to bring together, as the result of personal observation and experiment, all that can be said of the Yanadis as they are.

LIST OF REFERENCES.

Balmer, Lieutenant. Letter to Mr. Dykes, Collector of Nellore District, dated 22nd July 1865.

Boggs, Mrs. F. E. The Yanadis among the Telugus. Woman's Baptist Foreign Missionary Society, Tremont Temple, Boston

Boswell, Nellore District Manual. pp. 148-154.

Census Report, Madras. 1881. Vol. I p. 114.

Census Report, Madras 1891. Vol. XIII pp. 257-58.

Dykes, J. W B. Letter on the Yanadis, dated 31st July 1865

Gribble, J. D. B. Cuddapah Dist. Manual,

Chap. II Sec B, Population, p. 35.

Chap. XV Sec. I Forest and Hill Ranges, pp. 264-65.

Heinrichs, Rev. J. The Yanadis. The Baptist Missionary Review, pp. 450-56. November 1896.

Johnson, Cyclopædia. Articles on Ethnology and on the Yanans.

Keane, A. H. Ethnology. 1896.

Latham, R. L. Ethnology of India. 1859.

Man. The Andaman Islanders.

Macleane, C. D. The Madras Presidency Manual,

Vol I. (36.) 195.

Vol. II 7. 113.

Vol. III p. 1028.

Mullaly, F. S. Note on the Criminal classes of the Madras Presidency, pp. 21-27.

Shortt, Dr. An account of some rude tribes, the supposed aborigines of India. The Yanadis of Strihurreecotta 1864.

Statements of prisoners (including Yanadis) released from the District Jail Nellore and from the adjoining central jails as published in the Nellore District Gazette 1880-1894 (4 months excepted)

Stokes, H. E. Report on the Yanadis 1868.

Thurston, E. Madras Govt. Museum Bulletion, Vol. II No. 3.

Topinard. Anthropology.

THE YANADIS OF SOUTHERN INDIA.

The Yanadis are a long-headed, broad and concave-nosed, dark-skinned, short-statured tribe, inhabiting the Telugu speaking districts of the Madras Presidency, except Bellary. Their number was returned as 88,988 at the census of 1891 against 66,099 in 1881. 57,525 persons resided in 1891 in the Nellore district.

The word 'yanadis' has been subjected to much etymological speculation. *Firstly,* some derive it from *Anadulu* (అనాదులు), *a,* not and adi, beginning, people without a beginning. *Secondly,* others derive it from Anadhalu (అనాథలు), *a,* privative, and (sk) Natha, a lord or protector. The word is also said to mean 'unlording' or 'not lording,' *i.e.,* not included in the ruling or principal caste. *Thirdly,* it is also derived from *yanadamu* (Tel) యానాదము, sea-shore, or more precisely from *yanamu* (యానము), boat or wandering, and 'adi' (అది), means. Thus, the name was derived, as in similar cases, from their profession, which was wandering or living by boats on the sea-shore. *Fourthly,* vulgar usage and a rule of Telugu Grammar are relied on for converting the privative A and E into YA and YE, and for inserting the letter N for the sake of euphony after YA, the first syllable, and before the final syllable *Adi,* beginning. Thus the word means either 'without beginning' which is absurd, or 'not from the beginning' which is more probable. The Yanadis are therefore not the aborigines, but exotics; they are post-Dravidian and post-Aryan. This theory further relies on Bishop Caldwell's work on "Comparative Grammar of the Dravidian languages," which points out that the aboriginal tribes in Southern and Western Australia use almost the same words for I, thou, he, we, you, etc., as the Dravidian fishermen on the Madras Coast, and resemble in other ways, the Madras hill-tribes, as in the use of their national weapon, the boome-rang. *Fifthly*, from the last derivation, another hypothesis is, that the Yanadis, besides not belonging to the indigenous races of Southern India, were subsequent immigrants from some island or other continent, and that they had been ship-wrecked and stranded on the Nellore Coast, where they are principally found. They were originally either Negritos from the Straits settlements, or were from the East Coast of Africa or from South-west Australia, but they bear very striking resemblance to the Somalis at Aden. *Sixthly*, annotating this last theory, the Editor of the Baptist Mission Review suggests a probable connection between the Yanadis of Southern India and the Yanans of North California. The Yanans are a North American tribe, who differ from the other Indian tribes of California in physique and language, and who by tradition went from the Far East to California.

The above theories are hardly adequate or tenable. The first does not account for the appearance of N. The unenviable name of Anadhalu (అనాథలు) or protector-less or poor applies with stronger force to other tribes, and why this generic term was exclusively given to the Yanadis is not clear. The derivation from *yanadamu* or from *yanam* and *adi* is more fanciful than appropriate; the Yanadis were never known to have plied boats, and even if they did, there are none now on the boat-service on the East Cost canal, nor even at Sriharikota, still the head-quarters of the tribe. The exotic theory involved in the last of the etymological explanations is rather far-fetched. It is hardly in keeping with the natural pride of a race or tribe to be known by a name which indicates what they are not. The points of resemblance between the Australian and the Dravidian languages are many; the ethnic characteristics, skull formation, features, wavy-curled hair present similarities of type; but that the Yanadis along with the other tribes were therefore exotics from the localities named is a theory hardly tenable. The question is still in the air, and it is probable that the Australian and the Yanadi tribes both sprang from a main branch of the human race. According to Topinard, the Yanadis can only be said to bear striking resemblance, not so much to the Somalis in Aden, but to some black tribes, not Negro, with smooth hair mingled particularly among the Somalis; these black tribes are now extinct there, and it is probable that both they and the Yanadis were of the same stock. The caste is regularly established in India, but is found in a rudimentary state in Australia. According to Keane, the boomerang, unless locally evolved in Australia, must have been introduced from India. The theory of the two tribes, so widely separated from each other, springing from a main branch, or of the Australians being immigrants, is more in accord with evidence than that the Yanadi is an exotic from Australia or Africa. The suggestion contained in the annotation referred to above in no manner supports the exotic theory. The word Yanan (yaa-nan) means, in the language of the tribe, the people; it is chiefly known to the settlers by the name of Noje or Noji. Their tradition is that they went to California from the Far East. Their physical traits are singular. Their language is peculiar. Their population in 1884 was small, only 3[illegible]. These facts indicate that the tribe were exotics in California, and whatever connection may be traced between them and the Yanadis, it does not prove that the latter were exotics in India.

The more correct etymology seems to be న + ఆది, న being privative. According to Sanskrit Sandhi, the word would take the form of అనాది. Literally the expression means 'no beginning,' but the common acceptation of the term is, 'whose beginning is not traceable.' Temples, the origin of which is not known, are known as అనాదిస్థలం, *Anadi Sthalam.* The Yanadis are a Telugu-speaking tribe, their native language was no other. The Telugu they use is of the old pure dialect, and no admixture. The tribe must have been the aboriginal inhabitants of the Telugu province of India; the exotic theory does not stand to reason. The word *yanadi* appears to be a corruption of the Sanskrit term 'anadi.' The change cannot be accounted for by any rule of grammar. The law of *a* changing into *ya* (అ into య) does not apply to the first letter of any clause or phrase. When the Aryans pushed to the south and found the people there, they very naturally called them అనాదులు. Either through inability to pronounce correctly or because of their natural and peculiar intonation by elongating the vowel sounds, the peoples called themselves అనాదులు (Anadulu) or యానాదులు (Yanadulu).

They have their own vague traditions. Some speak of a flood in which only one man and one woman, their progenitors, were saved. Some say they are the aborigines of the wilds in the vicinity of the Pulicat lake, where they hunted and fished at will, till they became enslaved by the Reddies. Others say that the Reddi (*manchi*-good) Yanadis, a small but superior class, came from the mountains in the west, but were really originally Chenchus, fleeing from oppression and violence, and that they gradually amalgamated with the common Yanadis. The Chenchus are a sub-division of the tribe, and the Chenchudevata is their deity.

In physique, the average Yanadi is below middle height, dark-skinned, of bad odour, poor attenuated frame, with narrow chest and shoulders. His tribal costume is but a languti, and in rare cases a scrap of cloth round his waist. The female is ordinarily in rags, which she pieces together sufficiently to cover her body.

The average height of the men, according to my observations, is 162·56 cm., and of the women 147·82. They are generally long-limbed. As in the case of the Paniyans of Malabar, the average length of their feet (25·40 cm) largely exceeds the average breadth of the hips (21·59), and the difference of 3·81 cm., is by far greater than that of ·7 cm., which is considered to be a record figure for the Paniyans. The average nasal index is as high as 89·9, and indicates the Yanadi to belong to the jungle tribe. The cephalic index of a Yanadi recently placed before me for trial on a charge of dacoity is 75, and if this be accepted as the average record, the Yanadis, can be bracketted with the Lambadis, the Kurubas, and the Irulas. The average relative to stature of the distance from the middle finger to patella in 6·25. The span of arms relative to stature is 103·13, much as in the case of the Kotas and the Koramas.

The measurements of the under-trial prisoner placed for dacoity are :—

	cm.		Yanadi average.
Height	158·75	... ...	162·56.
Nasal height	4· 3	... ...	5·08.
Nasal breadth	3·91	... ...	3·81.
Nasal index	97	... ...	88·9.
Cephalic length	15·24		
„ breadth	11·43		
„ index	75		
Bigoniac	6·25		
Zygomatic	7·20		
Maxillo-Zygomatic index.	87		

The skull of an old Yanadi, aged 70 years, who died only a few weeks ago, gives the following measurements :—

		cm.
Longest portion of the skull		1[illegible]·69
Broadest portion of the skull		13·7
From one joint of the lower jaw to the other, over the lips.		20·85
From the joint of the lower jaw to the angle.		5·08
Frontal	(Tape)	12·07
Parietal	„	13·34
Occipital	„	10·80
Orbital breadth	„	4·23
Orbital height	„	2·80

The Yanadis have no valuable implemental or monumental materials to present to the student of research. The only implement is the boome-rang, and the only monument is his hut which has preserved its native shape. The only safe material available is the Yanadi himself. The animistic and, to some extent, the Zoo-theistic nature of his religion, the production of fire even at this date by the *Adivi* (forest) Yanadis by friction, the primitive hunting and fishing stage in which a large number of Yanadis are yet found to remain, and the almost raw animal food which they eat by simply heating or scorching the flesh of the game they hunt—these indicate that the Yanadis have not yet emerged from the Palæolithic stage of culture. They derive their names mainly from gods or goddesses and occasionally from ancestors. Their skin-color is more accurately speaking, dark-brown. They bathe but once a week and send forth from their skin distasteful odour. The development of the hairy system on the face or over the body generally is meagre; there is a good crop of curly hair on the head, and a slight strip of hair on the abdomen; the hair of the head is in colour from light-brown to black. They have dark-eyes, long-shaped faces, concave noses viewed in profile, prominent cheek-bones. The Yanadi on trial before me has thick lips, and prognathous lower jaw.

Summary of physical characteristics:—dolichocephalic; prognathous; leiotrichi, hairy system meagre, scanty moustache, no whiskers, scanty beard, slight strip of hair on the abdomen, colour of hair light brown to black; chin pointed; lips rather thick; high nasal index; men lanky and looking rather tall; long but poor-limbed, and frame attenuated; color of skin dark in men, and dark to brown in women; rather great dental wear with intelligence, consequently, in inverse ratio; muscle soft and flabby; men bow-shinned with muscles of calf slightly developed; average weight rather low.

Topinard places the Yanadis among the remnants of the Black strata out of the population of the Indian peninsula, the

Bhils, Mahairs, Ghonds and Khonds at the present time shut up in Central India, and with Maravars, Kurumbars, Veddahs etc., remaining in the south. Dr. Macleane places them among hill-tribes considered Tamulian or belonging to a stage later than the hill-tribes and the tribes remaining in the plains considered Tamulian. The evidences, slight as they are, of their primitive Palæolithic stage of culture support the aboriginal theory of the Yanadis, while the exotic theory was found not to have been satisfactorily established.

The island of Sriharikota in the Coramandel coast of the Nellore district is their head-quarters. It came into the possession ot Government in 1835, when the condition of the Yanadis first attracted notice. Proximity to the coast appears to have suggested the theory of ship-wreck and immigration, but the extensiveness of the forest in which they were found, added to characteristics which they in common with other tribes possess, point to them as a native hill-tribe. Their condition in 1835 was but one remove from savagery; they were not able to account how or when they went there; according to tradition, the Nabobs of former days left them there, and they lived an exclusive life, living on jungle produce. Their population was only 199. The Government undertook to ameliorate their condition by accepting from them the jungle products and assigning to them 20 per cent of their value in the shape of grain. The assignment was increased to 40 and even to 66·66 per cent in 1845. The products were sold by auction, and each person was given paddy, clothing and tobacco, equal in value to two-thirds of what was presented. In 1855, this system was changed to one of payment, partly in kind and partly in money. The change induced the Yanadis to extend their labors to collecting charcoal and felling timber. Parents received from Government two annas and six pies on the birth of every male child, and one anna, three pies for every female child—a bounty on productivity justified by special and local causes. A school with 50 childern was started in 1858 for teaching Telugu, under a teacher on ten rupees per mensem, who was given an assistant in 1861. Children were attracted by offers of paddy and clothing, made at first yearly, and subsequently converted into daily payments. An industrial department was added to teach basket-making. Some land was granted for cultivating chey-root. But the industries proved unsuccessful and the strength of the school went down. The school was finally abolished in 1877.

The Sriharikota Yanadis are considered to be the true Yanadis—they confine themselves to that island. They resemble the Villies of the adjoining district of Chingleput. They are extremely filthy in habits as evidenced by their skin and clothes, and they send forth a sickening odour which becomes stronger by perspiration. Their habits and sports, ceremonies and superstitions, will be noted in the sequel.

Their total population, according to the census 1891 (88.988), shows an increase of 34·61 per cent over the figure for 1881 (66,099). In Nellore, they are much more numerous than elsewhere, the corresponding increase being 45 per cent; 20,000 in 1865, 39,645 in 1881, 57,525 in 1891. The Telugu division, comprising all districts except Bellary, contained a population of 79,476 in 1891, the Agency division 3,321 and the Tamil division in Chingleput and Madras 2,191. In the Nellore district, over 50 per cent of the population are found in the two taluqs of Nellore and Gudur.

During the census of 1891, they returned 89 sub-divisions of which the Chenchu (5999) and the Manchi are numerically important. The other main and sub-divisions evidently differ in name alone; no well-marked differences exist. The tribe is divided into classes, following their dietary, profession or residence.

There are the Reddi, the Challa or Chatla, the Adivi, the Nakkala, the Kappala or the frog-eaters, and the non-frog eaters. The Reddi Yanadis are a settled race employed chiefly as cooks by the Panta (cultivating) Reddis. They do not mingle with the Challa and the Adivi Yanadis whom they look upon as outcastes. The Challa Yanadis are known by other names—Garappa, (dry-land), and Chatla (tree). They reside in huts on the borders of the village, living on jungle produce, snaring and hunting game, and working for the villagers. These Reddi and Challa Yanadis are occasionally employed as Kavalgars or village watchmen in the Kistna and the Godavari districts. The Adivi Yanadis, as the name indicates, are jungle wallahs, the true nomads, the houseless wanderers, who are professional burglars out of the Nellore district. The Nakkala Yanadis in the south of the Ganjam district, and in the upland taluqs of the Godavari and Vizagapatam districts are scattered gangs deriving their name from their habit of snaring and eating jakals. They call themselves Toorpu or East Yanadis, but are not acknowledged by their southern brethren. The Manchi or good Yanadis are a small and superior class, who came down from the mountains and amalgamated themselves with the common Yanadis. Between these and the Chenchu Yanadis, there is some connection. The Yanadis of the North Arcot district, who worship the deity of Chenchu, are known as the Chenchu Yanadis. They are non-frog eaters, and will not suffer the Kappala or frog-eating Yanadis even to touch their pots. The frog-eaters are confined to the Nellore district. The Chenchu Yanadis are divided into gangs of about 200 or 300, each under a headman. There are also the refuse-eaters and those who do not eat refuse in the Nellore district. In the Kavali Taluq of this district, there are the Somari or the idle Yanadis.

The Yanadis have no tribal marks or party badges, nor have they symbols of rank or status among them. They consider themselves "caste people" and as a sub-division of the Sudras, much superior to the Pariahs or the Malas and the Madigas, in whose houses they will not eat. There appears to be some principle even in refuse-eating; the Chinna Yanadi vandlu or the refuse-eaters will not eat of the refuse of

Mondibandavandlu, Voddas, Yerukalas, Malas, Madigas, Christians etc. To do so is excommunication, which is pronounced by a Balijasetti, whose decision on such matters is binding. The excommunicated person can be admitted to society only after passing through an ordeal, after which he should feed a number of caste Yanadis. His tongue is scalded by the Balijasetti with hot gold and he becomes pure. He promises never more to repeat the sin.

The patriarchal system obtains to some extent. The elders are looked upon as natural leaders and authorities. They had always their headmen. The headman is called కులంపెద్ద or పెద్దయానాది or maistry. He has powers over the group to which he belongs. At present there is a headman for every twenty huts. He can excommunicate, he can impose and collect fines, or remit them of his own will or on the recommendation of a body of their castemen. The hereditary head of the tribe at Sriharikota at one time wielded immense influence, but his office is now more or less honorary and nominal.

They adopt house-names which indicate both the purity and the impurity of the blood. కత్తి (Kathi), పాముల (Pamula), తుపాకుల (Tupakula), మేకల (Mekala), యాకశిరి (Yakasiri), పులి (Puli) are pure-Yanadi house-names, but తిరుమలశెట్టి (Tirumala-setti), తిరువీధి (Tiruveedi), శిద్దపరెడ్డి (Sithapareddi), రాచగిరి (Ra-chagiri) indicate hybrid origin, the children adopting the house-names of the non-tribe men with whom the mothers had evidently lived.

Their dietary includes bandy coots, rats, cats, crabs, jackals and excludes beef. They eat flesh more or less raw, only scorching or heating but not roasting it.

They speak Telugu of the old pure dialect, a little corrupt, with an elongated sound, "probably a drawling pronunciation of the long vowels." They not merely elongate, but even shorten the long vowels at times. They are not like the

Yerukalas, who speak a mixture of Tamil and Telugu, irrespective of locality. A few, who reside or have settled in the Tamil districts speak Tamil, but with Telugu words mixed. Such is not the case with the Telugu spoken by the Yanadis.

Their ideas of religion are of the rudest and most primitive nature. Their objects of worship include stones and bricks set up in a retired place near their hut and sprinkled with a red powder. A pot filled with water in which margossa leaves are steeped, is also kept up for worship. They worship also the village goddess or the grama devata. A దేవరయిల్లు or house of the god is set apart in certain localities. No pollution is allowed into it. They draw images of gods on the wall and worship the same with red powder and flowers; the worship is known as గోడపూజ or wall-worship. They sometimes daub a tree with saffron &c., and sing in its praise. They have no separate temples; they are their own priests. *Chenchu Devudu* is the name of their house-hold deity, which is generally worshipped under the form of a handful of clay, squeezed and put upon a small platform of earth under an Aruka tree, which they consider as sacred. In Sriharikota the deity is a wooden idol. Probably Chenchu Devudu was once a hero or a renowned ancestor, and in this matter of ancestor-worship, the Yanadis resemble the Kurumbas. The pious worship, offer flowers, cooked rice &c., performing the ceremony every Friday; in Sriharikota, the Yanadis worship once or twice a month. The ordinary Yanadi worships only on occasions of marriages, funerals and the like. During worship, a Yanadi sometimes gets possessed, answers queries, and is sought for information. The belief is that a spirit is in him and speaks through him. Animal sacrifice is offered to goddesses Poleramma and Ankamma of local significance, but during the worship of Chenchu the devotees abstain from animal food and take only one meal of roots or fruits every day. They worship also Subbaroyudu (the serpent-god), Venkatesvarulu, Penchala Narasimhulu and other local gods, whose images in clay are exhibited in the. దేవరయిల్లు or house of god. Camphor and frankincense are burnt, fruits, dhal &c., are offered and distributed.

According to the latest census, 84,439 persons were Hindus and 549 animists. If the classification was based on the information of the Yanadis or of the enumerators themselves, it is difficult to accept the figures. It may be that their religious rites were copied from or resemble the usages of the Hindus—wearing marks, offering sacrifices, and calling themselves Vaishnavites and Saivites as the Hindus do—but it is a fact, still that in order to exalt their own deities they almost universally adopt, methods of worship, giving supernatural powers to, and, endowing with life and mind, inanimate objects and the spirits of geographical features. They are animists and zoo-theists as well. Their gods are mainly influenced by dancing and music and also by a variety of crude ceremonies.

Christian Missionaries have now taken them up. " At Ramapatam, a large amount of patience, persuasion, prayer and faith had to be exercised in the bargain. The children are not now bribed to come to school or to Church, but they have to be given a free education including board and clothing, if they come." In the early forties, the Government undertook to ameliorate the physical condition of the Yanadi; in the closing years of the century, the American Baptist Mission are earnest in their attempt to capture his body and soul together. A few Yanadis are already members of this Church, " not indeed very faithful in the discharge of their duties "—it is difficult to expect the primitive Yanadi to be—" but still enlisted in the cause of Christ." There are at this date compositors, teachers, and preachers of the making of the American Baptist Mission, who are zealous both at civilising and Christianising them.

The Yanadi marriage is based on the consent of the parties, the elders rarely intervening. Seduction is visited by the girl's parents on the head of the male with punishment, but if the girl prefers, she is permitted to live with him. If they elope for a time, they are man and wife. Maturity precedes marriage, but early marriage is an exception. The marriage ceremony is often avoided on account of expense. The Adivi Yanadis as a rule avoid, but the Reddi Yanadis always observe it. Where there is a ceremony, there is betrothal at the bridegroom's, invitation of friends and distribution of betel and nuts, which complete the marriage. The Yanadis have of late borrowed largely the customs of the Sudras,—consulting purohits, fixing the time of marriage, making presents, bathing the couple, tying the thali &c. Brahmins do not officiate at their marriages, but their place is taken by the bride's maternal uncle. In regular marriages, the bridegroom first obtains the consent of the bride's maternal uncle by bribing or presenting him with eight annas. The bride's father gets a suit of clothing, two cloths to wear, one to cover the body, and another for the head. The bride's mother gets two cloths to wear. Guests assemble, the couple bathe and wear new cloths dyed in saffron, the kankanam or talisman, a cotton thread in the place of betel leaf now out of fashion, is tied to the right wrist, as a sort of absolution from defilement, and the tali is tied as a marriage symbol at the right time. The auspicious hour is the noon, which is determined by a pole two feet high fixed perpendicularly on a level piece of ground erected for the marriage. Formerly an arrow symbolical of the Yanadis' hunting proclivities, or an imitation made out of the screw pine, used to be fixed. The bridegroom and the bride stand at either end of the platform, and the thali is tied when the auspicious hour thus indicated has arrived. The marriage symbol for the Yanadis was for a long time the flower of the Tangedu (*Cassa Auriculata*), but the bottu is now manufactured in gold by a goldsmith, and is taken from his house in a procession with drum and dance. After tying the thali, the couple pour sacred rice over each other's heads. This rice goes to the maternal uncle, in addition to the present he has already received. The bridegroom then feasts the whole marriage-party. He also pays in kind and in coin for the music and the drum, supplied by professional Yanadis. The pair enjoy honey-moon under the roof of the bride's parents, one month after marriage.

Widowhood does not involve disfigurement. Widows can remarry, but as a rule no ceremony is observed. The widow continues to wear the mark and is at liberty to take one after another as many as seven husbands. The larger the number of husbands, the higher is her place in society and her title to decide disputes such as those arising from adultery and the like. Verily a veteran judge! Adultery is no serious offence among the tribe, and widows live in concubinage. The Yanadis are by nature jealous of conjugal rights, but in practice excuse adultery by exacting a bribe if the wives' parents can afford. Divorces are easily obtained. The deserted wife joins her new husband with her children, but he is not bound to protect them. I have known of instances where the husbands and wives and their children lived together, while the children of previous matrimony were thrown on the world. Polygamy is common, but polyandry never. A Yanadi has as many as seven wives, but he houses them separately and lives with them by turns.

Pregnancy before marriage is not objectionable. The women generally attain puberty at the age of fourteen, and the child-bearing age ranges from sixteen to forty-five. As a class they beget several children, barrenness being scarce. The table (iii) at the end proves the fecundity of the Yanadis.

The maternal uncle plays an important part not merely at the marriage, but at the head-shaving ceremony of the lad of five—not a primitive custom, but another instance of borrowing. As the guests assemble and feast, he plucks off one lock of hair from his head and ties it to a bough of the Aruka tree. He receives a present of a measure of rice, a new cloth, and eight annas, and the head is then clean shaved. The lad is taken to a spot dedicated to goddess Ankamma or Poleramma, to whom a fowl is offered. In the evening, they light torches and indulge in wild dances.

There is hardly any pollution following child-birth. For three days after delivery, the women live on the tender leaf, bed or cabbage of the date plant (*Phœnix Sylvestrus*), after which they take rice &c. The mother usually bathes on the tenth day. Margossa leaves, sometimes the leâves of other trees, and the knife with which the umbilical cord is cut are placed under the child's head for six days. They hang a net in front of the door to keep the demous out, and do not sweep the house for some days. The child is not named for a month or even longer. The parents take the child to a soothsayer who pretending to be possessed of this god or that goddess says give my name,' and that is settled.

The Yanadis make-believe that they can prophesy destinies, hold interviews with gods and goddesses, and interpose between god and man to purge the latter of his sins. They resemble the Nilgiri Kurumbas in this respect. They call themselves soothsayers, only one or two persons setting themselves as such for a village. The art of soothsaying is learnt under tuition from an expert. The pupil isolates himself in a closed hut and remains in meditation for a fortnight, abstaining from all cooked food, and feeding on milk, fruit &c. In time he gets sight of a shadowy form or a goddess, and feels inspired. The form tells him that he or she is either Ankamma, Poleramma, Venkateswarulu, Subbaroyudu or Malakondrayadu. The devotee burns camphor and frankincense. His pupilage has ceased. He sings to the deity. The master and the pupil take a sea-bath; the latter makes an offering of cooked food consisting of rice and dhal, and he becomes an independent soothsayer. Times were when the ardent pupil used his hand instead of the wooden spoon for stirring boiling rice with. The real soothsayer now invokes the gods with burning charcoal in folded hands under beat of drum.

The soothsaying is called "rangam pattee" in Noth Arcot, and "Sodi" *i. e.*, truth, in Nellore. The soothsayer keeps a separate house, the దేవరయిల్లు, Devara house or house of God, which we have already noticed. The local gods are exhibited in it in clay, especially the tribal deity *Chenchu devudu.* The house is always kept clean; there is regular worship, and distribution of dhal and jaggary. Fridays, Saturdays, and Sundays are auspicious days for soothsaying. The male is the chief soothsayer. The applicant presents him with betel, nuts and money. The soothsayer bathes and sits; his wife or some other female kindles a fire and throws frankincense into it. He beats his drum and sings, and a woman from within repeats every sentence in a shrill voice. The songs are but salutations in praise of the deities at whose and the soothsayer's feet the applicant has fallen, invoking aid. The soothsayer then appears inspired and addresses the supplicant in terms such as these: "You neglected to worship me. I shall ruin you if you do not propitiate me in a befitting manner" and predicts in song his good or bad fortune. This is believed and acted upon.

The Yanadis invariably bury their dead, but Dr. Shortt noticed in 1865 some corpses subjected to cremation. They are afraid that the spirit of the departed would catch them and hence, often forsake a place where a death has occurred, especially a death from cholera. Their funeral rites are more or less similar to those observed by some of the Hindus. They observe the చిన్నదినము or small day, sprinkling a little milk and water over the grave on the second or the third day after death. Cooked rice is also thrown, and if it is eaten by crows, the deceased has been propitiated; it should not be polluted by dogs, but cows can eat it. Pollution is observed by the Sapindas or close consanguinity until the పెద్దదినం or grand funeral, which is celebrated some day after the 9th according to convenience, preferably on a Wednesday. A lump of clay representing the deceased is put up and worshipped, and the people dance around it. The male consanguinity shave and bathe. There is feasting, dancing and soothsaying. By the way, the soothsayers smear one half of their face with different colors,—black, white and red. The coast-land Yanadis take a sea-bath while the others bathe at home, and the purification is then complete. As a rule, a responsible member from every family in close consanguinity with the deceased attends the funeral. They remove the dead, bury and bathe, and the Gothrapuvaru or Sapindas drink a handful of water (దోసిడిదప్పి తాగుతారు). Those who keep the house of god keep clear of those that are polluted.

Their education is at the lowest ebb. Their mental calibre is at the lowest point. The special efforts taken by the Government at Sriharikota to give them elementary education and to train them to habits of useful industry proved a failure, notwithstanding that the school was maintained for some 20 years at considerable expense. Nor are the efforts of the Missionaries in this direction eminently successful. According to the census of 1891, only 230 persons out of a population of 84,988 were learning and literate, while 82,385 were illiterate; nothing is stated of the remaining 2373. Some can count up to 16, while only a few of these can go up to 36.

For a long time, until the early thirties when their degraded savagery attracted the attention of the Government, they were simple collectors of jungle produce, more or less feeding on them, working at will but being under no restraint. They were not accustomed to servitude, having roamed for ages free over the hills or in the forests, but when these were brought under control, they felt the pinch, as they were not accustomed to work and to earn under restrictions. Their laziness remains with them, and it is notoriously true even to this day that it is easier to educate the Yanadi than to tempt him to work for any wage, if he is sure of his next meal. But even in want, he avoids the Famine Relief Works which attract all other classes, for the simple reason that he is loth to place himself under restrictions. There are a very few Yanadis in police service as constables, Some are kavalgars; some farm-servants, menials and scavengers. A number of them are faithful domestic servants. They own neither land nor animals. They are not known to remain constant in their profession, except perhaps as domestic servants. They earn their livelihood by a variety of ways—by hunting, fishing, cobra-charming, gathering honey, picking fuel, rearing and selling pigs, practising medicine and the like, and in rare cases by thieving. But they are not steady at anything, being proverbially lazy, and it is no surprise that short commons is their permanent tale of woe. Their poor frames and bony bodies evidently prove that they do not generally know what a full or a double meal is like.

But they are men of hard endurance, working or walking several hours at a stretch without food, and in this respect they present a marked contrast to the aboriginal Andamanese, who cannot abstain from food without inconvenience, for more than eight hours at a time, and who, not being able to endure privation in respect to drink, take always with them a supply of fresh water in bamboo vessels called *gob*. They are a contented lot, furnishing cheap labour, never caring for the morrow, indulging themselves in their native dances, always preferring freedom to servitude. Sometimes, they enter into contracts, but in their low and uneducated state, they do not feel bound to fulfil them. They live in low cone-shaped huts which afford protection from the sun and the shower, but generally they cook, eat and sleep without. The huts are rude frame-works of bamboo and twig and palmyra leaf, at the greatest 7 feet high, with small entrances through which men have only to crawl. They are filthy and untidy in habits; the men do not wash themselves oftener than once a week, while the women do so probably twice a week or once a day. The Yanadis are their own quacks and treat other classes as well. They are more successful than others, for the simple reason that experience teaches them the efficacy of several herbs and roots with which they come across. They are less dangerous than ordinary quacks, as they invariably use vegetable and not any mercurial or poisonous drugs. Among themselves, they trust to Nature's cure for ordinary indispositions. The Yanadi women take no medicine ordinarily at child-birth, but drink a decoction in special cases of ailment. The Yanadis offer to treat for rheumatism, paralysis, fevers and the like. They are terribly afraid however of cholera, for which they have no cure. They run away from cholera-affected localities, neglecting their own cholera-stricken relations. I noticed a woman of good physique and strong build suffering from cholera, and in the cold and last stage, lying neglected by the side of a brook. Her parents, her husband, her brothers and sisters all forsook her, but an affectionate family dog kept company in her last moments. The woman lay bleeding at the mercy of fishes at the water's edge. I administered two dozes of Lorbeer's cholera mixture, but she brightened up only to die. A Yanadi man in service absolutely refused to carry with me a bottle of disinfectant to a locality where his own nearest relation lay dead of cholera. They use drugs for snake-bite and scorpion-sting, with not always successful results. They are experts not so much at curing the bite as at charming the cobra. They catch cobras fearlessly and without removing fangs, letting their hands into a hole and dragging them out. They would have believe that they succeed through incantations, but probably they are able to keep the cobras as if under spell through will-force or animal magnetism. They are good guides in forests and over hills, they are good shikaris and excellent shots. They are fearless in the jungle, hardly ever weary, quick and sure-footed in climbing over mountains, and they know best the spots where the different animals resort during particular seasons. Same Yanadis in the Venkatagiri Zamindary have taken licenses under the Arms Act, and in the Venkatagiri forest, which is full of game, they are known to bag tigers, hunt cheetas, porcupines and other wild animals.

The Yanadi dance is indicative of merry life, men, women, and children indulging in it. They dance during ceremonies and occasionally for begging, coloring the body with saffron and charcoal in stripes, wearing flowers, singing meaningless songs, and drumming rudely "dambukku, dambukku"; of late they have learnt to appear on the stage, enacting some Telugu dramas in public streets but only in the rudest fashion.

As a rule, the children of brothers and sisters do not marry; probably, this accounts for the maternal uncles of the bridegroom and the bride being important personages, receiving bribes and presents as a set off for their own children not being preferred. They have lately borrowed the custom of adopting children, but no ceremony is observed, no giving or taking in regular form and no changing of house names.

Those who can afford drink toddy and arrack. They take their own rice with them when they accept invitations for marriages, when they attend funerals, and when they meet for any ceremonies. They thus make very welcome guests; the host is none the worse, probably all the better, for their meeting and making merriment.

They are a happy contented people, and this, evidently because they have not risen much above the primitive stage. Their clothing is rather thread-bare. Their jewellery for the females is growing with modern fashion,—glass bangles for the wrist, brass kammalu for the ear, bulaki for the nose, and several other trifles in imitation. The males bore their noses. The children play hide and seek.

The Yanadis climb wonder-fully over difficult, almost inaccessible and perpendicular cliffs 100 to 200 feet high, to collect honey. The bees have their hive beside or below precipitious hill-tops, which the Yanadis reach by climbing with the help of a plaited rope made of young bamboos tied together. The rope is fastened on the top of the cliff by means of a peg driven into the ground or a tree. He climbs armed with a basket and a stick He swings suspended in the air. He burns some brushwood or grass under the hive; it drives ou a majority of the bees. Another swing takes him close to the hive, which he pokes with his stick. He receives the pieces of the hive into his basket and the honey which begins to flow into a vessel which he adjusts below. When the basket or the vessel is full, the Yanadi shakes the rope and is drawn up. His nearest relation, say his wife's brother, is in charge of the rope, and there is no fear of foul play. Considerable quantities of honey and wax are thus gathered, but the Yanadis probably get no more than their daily wages for their labours at perilous heights. The contractor makes enormous gains.

The Yanadis are usually classed along with professional criminal tribes, the Lambadis, the Yerukalas and the Dommaras, but they hardly deserve the odium. In the early years of police organisation, their utterly degraded and almost savage condition evidently furnished the detectives with a ready crop. In the sixties, Lieutenant Balmer, Superintendent of Police, Nellore district, considered them thieves and house-breakers, almost without exception; he remarked that almost every Yanadi would steal when he found an opportunity, and that they were the most determined and successful house-breakers and even dacoits. From the number of criminals which the tribe furnished, the official view was that they preponderated in crime over other wild tribes, and that the preponderance was due to "the radical viciousness of the race." The generalization was disputed even at that time on the ground of the superiority of the Yanadi numbers and of the more migratory habits of the other wild tribes, who defeated detection. All the same, later writers still held the tribe as criminal. In support of this rather one-sided theory, the Yanadis of Cuddapah are quoted as sheep-lifters and even murderers, but they form less than 5 per cent of the whole Yanadi population, and the offences are due more to the vice of the locality than to the viciousness of the race. The manual on the criminal castes of the Madras Presidency evidently deals with only some 10 per cent of the Yanadis living in the more northern districts;

the remarks smack of departmental over-drawn contributions. The compiler of the Madras Presidency Manual accepts on trust, for the entire tribe, conclusions which do not comprise over 15 per cent of the population. The Yanadis of North Arcot who number some 8 per cent are certified to be a "simple and truthful people." The Rev. Mr. Heinrichs considers them "skilful thieves themselves; they are adepts in detecting thieves, wherefore they are not infrequently employed by the police and others in detection;" but his range of observation was not wide. From the same locality, Mrs. F. E. Boggs of the same mission has a different story to give. "A casteman, a farmer living near Ramapatam, went early one morning to his straw, and discovered that some had been stolen. He immediately attacked an infirm old Yanadi man, accused him of the theft, and gave him a fearful beating with a heavy stick, over the bare neck." And again in stronger terms. "A most daring robbery of upwards of Rs. 500 worth of jewellery was committed in Ramapatam nearly 3 years ago (1891). It was believed to have been the work of one of the prominent, influential village officicials, but he succeeded in getting the charge fastened on two timid helpless Yanadi men. They were tried before a native Magistrate and, on the testimony of false witnesses, hired as we knew for the occasion, convicted and sent to jail. We believed the poor men innocent, and succeeded in having the case brought before an English Collector, who reversed the judgment and released the men, and they joyfully returned to their houses. But they and their families were persecuted and threatened by their enemies, who were angry at this turn of affairs, and for weeks dared not sleep in their own houses." Afraid of further bullying, one of the number said to Mrs. Boggs that they would sleep in the verandah of the mission buiding that she might "see that we men are all there, for our enemies are going to bring another charge against us, and we want you to know that we are all here every night, so you will be able to testify for us". "After living in this state of terror for weeks, they were hunted out of the place, and all the connected families moved away, about 150 miles distant, where they are still living."

The Yanadis of the Nellore district form over 67 per cent of the whole tribe. Statistics give an average of 135 criminals for the five years ending April 1865, and a mean of 129 for the years 1865 and 1867. The method of recording criminal statistics has considerably changed. The number of Yanadis of the district released from the Nellore district jail and from central jail for a period of 15 years (less by four months) was 637. These related to somewhat graver offences dealt with by the Magistrates of the district. The figure does not include releases from the sub-jails, but these would not have been many; there were several cases of less than one-month imprisonments taken into the district jail. At any rate, taking the number of offences for which they have been condemned as a class to be approximately accurate, the average for a year is 44·44 for a population of 57525 or much less than 1 per mille. The total number of all classes for the same period was 3528 or an average of 244 every year, or 1·70 per mille of population. Thus the average against the Yanadi is considerably less than that against the total population for the district. And how much less would it be, if the statistics furnished an accurate idea of the really criminal Yanadis! Mrs. Boggs' picture is not over-drawn. The Yanadi is a meek creature, an ignorant and a degraded man, who does not know what it is to cross-examine, who cannot make out the proceedings of the court, who is not aware that he has the right of defence, and who submits as a matter of course to the ordeal which sends him to prison. No witnesses are generally willing to speak in his favor. He is in dread of the police, and witnesses who know the truth are not willing to make enemies. When offences are registered, they must be detected, and it sometimes happens that police caps are found to fit Yanadi heads, better than others'; without the slightest ado. And the joinder of offences, house-breakings of all sorts with thefts, is almost always a manipulation which the prosecutor knows best how to make on the most slender data. Even these data are often more imaginary than real. The joinder affair is thus at times a fiction, making the less grave appear the more serious. The proper average, if the Yanadi dealt with his case as well as the Yerukala or the Dommara, would be much below the present figure. I myself tried cases in which the Dommara cross-examined witnesses in a manner likely to throw the best counsel into the shade, whereas the Yanadi stood like a mummy, leaving his business to be done by me. It is due to the Yanadi to state that in a large percentage of the prosecutions, he only answers for the sins of others. Of the 637 cases referred to, 15 were for dishonestly receiving stolen property knowing it to be such, 6 for giving false evidence, 6 for hindering or assaulting a constable on duty, 5 for theft as servants, 9 for breach of contract, 3 for criminal appropriation, 4 (of whom 3 were females) for attempting to commit suicide, 1 for exposure of a child for abandonment, 2 for hurt, 2 for grievous hurt and 13 for robberies and dacoities; of the remainning, a large number were house-breakings and thefts under one section of the code or another. Evidently, the Yanadi does not know what it is to appeal, and even if he does, the chances are against him because of the strong record made up in the court below. Under the Penal Code, the essence of an offence lies in intention, but it can hardly be said that in a large number of these cases the ignorant Yanadi deliberately committed the offence. Making every allowance for the ignorance, meekness and the degraded condition of the Yanadi, considering the extraordinary tactics of his prosecutors, who require some body,—better if he is the actual offender,—to confess, to admit, or by hook or crook to go to jail and thus help to close the record, taking these into cousideration, the criminal average goes down and the odium varnishing the tribe wears away.

The infinitesimal average cannot brand the tribe as a whole. There is the individual Yanadi criminal, as there is in every clan, class, tribe. He commits thefts, as every man in want does, but he does not on that account bring discredit to his class. He is no criminal by instinct, he is no criminal by passion, he is no criminal from chance, he is no criminal from habit, but if he is one, he is so from necessity. He does not present any remarkable abnormities, such as a criminal anthropologist would expect to find in established criminals. The police records include in the K. D. lists several criminal gangs, such as the Yerukulas, the Kathiras, the Dommaras, but not the Yanadis. Individual Yanadis may figure there, but that is not the point. If the conclusions, which the statistics published for the Nellore district warrant, can be taken to apply for the tribe as a whole, the Yanadis are no criminal class. Considering their want, their ignorance, their degradation, their illiteracy and their meekness, they are a good, simple and faithful tribe. True, the Yanadi catches contagion and offers brass calling it gold; true, he purchases and promises, but does not always pay; but on the whole he is a mild man, a faithful servant, a degraded being, a simple person.

The Yanadis deserve the very best attention at the hands of the authorities, at the hands of the missionaries, and deserve better of their countrymen. They are useful servants, faithful and trustworthy. They should be cured of their lazy habits. They evoke pity, but while they grow the lazier for the false pitying, they become the brisker for the kindly whipping.